COUNTRY
CHURCHES

COUNTRY CHURCHES

Raymond Paul Zirblis

MetroBooks

MetroBooks

An Imprint of Friedman/Fairfax Publishers

©1998 by Michael Friedman Publishing Group, Inc.

Library of Congress Cataloging-in-Publication Data

Zirblis, Raymond Paul.
    Country churches / by Raymond Paul Zirblis.
        p.   cm.
    Includes bibliographical references and index.
    ISBN 1-56799-588-8
    1. Rural churches. 2. Church architecture. I. Title.
    NA4827.5.Z57   1998
    726.5—dc21   98-6289

Editor: Ann Kirby
Art Director: Jeff Batzli
Designer: Kirsten Wehmann Berger
Photography Editor: Sarah Storey
Production Manager/Director: Karen Matsu Greenberg

Color separations by Hong Kong Scanner Arts International Ltd.
Printed in Hong Kong by Midas Printing Limited
1 3 5 7 9 10 8 6 4 2
For bulk purchases and special sales, please contact:
Friedman/Fairfax Publishers
Attention: Sales Department
15 West 26th Street
New York, NY 10010
212/685-6610 FAX 212/685-1307

Visit our website:
http://www.metrobooks.com

Dedication

To my mother, with love and affection.

Contents

Chapter 1

Origins and Developments of Church Architecture

ountry churches—whether they are the simple stone churches that dot the landscape of rural Britain, the austere wood-framed houses of worship found in the towns and villages of New England, or the whitewashed adobe mission churches of the American Southwest— are humble structures compared to the huge, imposing cathedrals that are their counterparts in the major urban centers of Europe and elsewhere. Yet these simple structures have always had a far greater meaning for a far greater number of people than do those towering achievements of architectural genius.

Their charm derives in part from their very simplicity, for their unpretentious and utilitarian design reflects the central role they have always played in the daily lives of rural communities. These churches were not meant merely to inspire reverence in the minds of believers; rather, they are places where the members of small, close-knit communities could come together regularly to express their religious faith in common.

A plain sanctuary, a modest bell tower, and a surrounding churchyard are the basic elements of this familiar architectural type, sufficient to fulfill the spiritual needs of a rustic community. In a world where religion was an active and daily part of people's lives, and travel was generally limited to the local community, the village church was a familiar and comfortable place, visited weekly rather than only a few times a year. It was the setting for the stages of each individual's journey through life, the site of baptisms, marriages, burials, and other rites that gave support and meaning to existence.

A wayside chapel guarding an Austrian mountain pass in winter evokes a time when a journey beyond one's village called for divine protection, and the church and its symbols marked the safe path for this world and the next.

The country church was also a place to visit, gossip, do business, and go courting, as Sunday services were often the only occasions for which widely dispersed rural communities assembled. In many remote areas of Europe, this type of rural, church- and community-bound society existed with very little change from the early Middle Ages all the way up until World War II.

Most if not all country churches share a modesty of design and execution that reflects their central utilitarian role in rural societies. At the same time, of course, their specific architectural styles vary greatly, depending on the place and time of their construction. Styles and designs have been influenced by factors as mundane as the availability of construction materials and funding, and as abstract as the state of scholarly theological disputes. And, naturally, simple fashion has always played an important role.

Prayer and candle lighting remains a common daily or weekly devotional in the Catholic and Eastern Orthodox churches, as seen in this chapel in the Pindos mountains. Metsovo, Greece.

Early Churches

The evolution and diversification of church architecture mirrors that of Christianity itself, as it grew from a despised and persecuted sect within the Roman Empire to become one of the most widely practiced and greatly varied religions on earth.

In the third and fourth centuries A.D., Christians in Rome often met

in private homes and hired halls converted to serve as places of worship. During periods when persecution was at its most threatening, they even assembled among the remains of their ancestors in the catacombs beneath the city.

Private houses and other secret places of worship were common when Christians were a persecuted

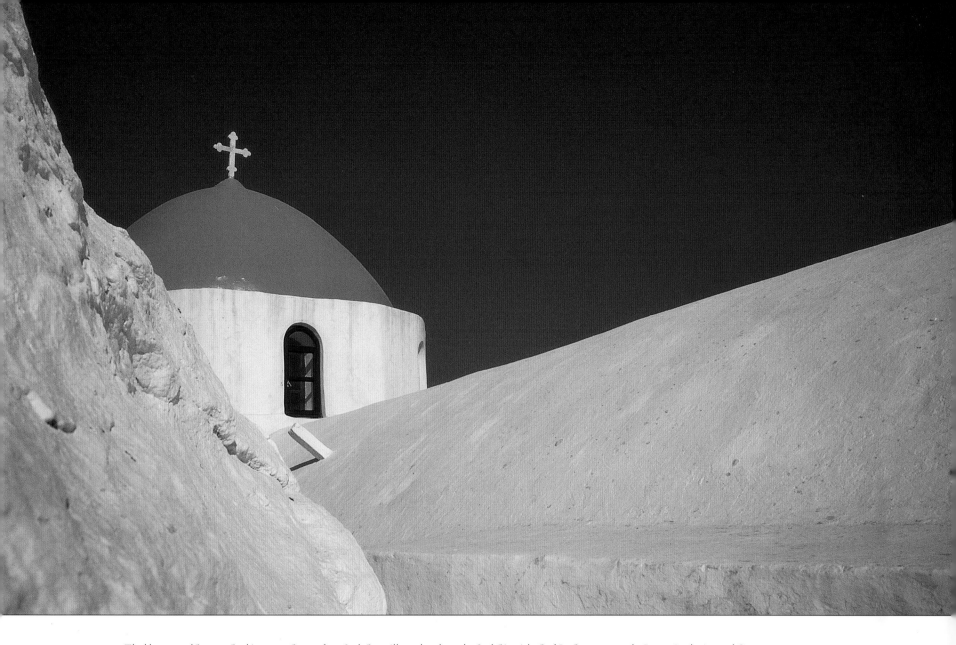

The blue central dome and white stucco drum of an Orthodox village church on the Cycladian island of Ios demonstrate the Byzantine heritage of Greece.

minority. However, once the emperor Constantine recognized Christianity in 324, making it the official religion of the Roman Empire, an official, public church building became necessary, one that was clearly distinct from the temples of Rome's pagan past. Two classic forms, the mausoleum and the basilica, provided the precedents for this new religious architecture. Mausoleums were commemorative tombs, round or polygonal in shape, with domed roofs, while basilicas were rectangular pillared meeting-halls. Both could easily be adapted to any size, and both have been used as models in the design of Christian places of worship ever since.

With the gradual division of the Roman Empire, the Christian church split as well, with resulting variations in church architecture. The Eastern Church commonly employed the circular mausoleum form with a domed roof, or at least combined the mausoleum's dome with the basic form of the basilica. These churches were usually laid out in the form of a Greek cross, with four arms of equal length, serving to focus attention upon a central point beneath the dome. Church structures in Russia, Greece, and parts of Eastern Europe continue to reflect this preference.

OPPOSITE: *From the mid-nineteenth to early twentieth centuries, immigrants to the United States often settled in tight-knit communities and erected local churches that affirmed their Old World heritage while embracing their new home. This Greek cross plan church with domed corner towers and central domed sanctuary was built by Romanian immigrants in Warren, Michigan.* ABOVE: *A rural town that could not afford a dome might achieve a similar visual effect in two dimensions, as in this church in Castilla-La-Mancha, Cuenca, Spain. The extended parapet is topped with a semi-circular pediment and lightened with a pair of round-arched openings that simulate windows.*

The stone basilica church at Andlau is seen here in spring, and is typical of rural Alsace, France.

In the West, on the other hand, the Christian Church adopted the basilica form with a simple pitched roof as the basic model for its places of worship. These churches tend to follow the plan of a Latin cross, with three short arms and a single long one, which encourages attention to be drawn to the focal point of the altar and sanctuary, with a long perspective emphasized by colonnades. In England, France, Spain, and their colonial offspring around the world, the basilica with pitched roof is still the very image of a church.

During the Middle Ages (roughly from the fall of the Roman Empire in the fifth century to the fifteenth century), sometimes referred to as the West's Dark Ages, the Church alone provided a sense of unity. Missionaries carried the Christian religion north and west, and the basilica design traveled with it. As adaptable to different local environments as was Christianity itself, the basilica church was built in local timber, brick, or stone. It was ideal either for a small parish church or for a grand cathedral.

In the years around 800 A.D., Charlemagne's empire, which stretched from northern Spain to eastern Germany, brought short-lived political unity to Western Europe for the first time since the collapse of the Roman Empire in 496. With it came a renaissance of art and learning, and a resurgence of church construction. Most of the churches erected in this building boom were humble parish structures in isolated villages, usually built of timber.

Stone soon became the preferred building material throughout Western Europe, but a tradition of timber churches survived, particularly in Eastern Europe and Scandinavia. Some twenty Norwegian stave churches, dating from the twelfthcentury and later, still stand today, and suggest what the lost early wood churches of Northern Europe must have been like. They are framed in heavy timber, and rise in tiers, each steep roof clad with wooden shingles.

The early medieval Lom Stave Church at Jotunheimen, Norway, is a masterwork of Northern European woodcarving and joinery, erected around 1100 A.D. Seen here from the churchyard, the cross plan and round apse are Southern European features, but the gables support dragon heads. Reminiscent of the figureheads of Viking ships, these come from pagan tradition and may have been meant to drive away evil spirits.

Romanesque Churches

The Romanesque style developed in the second half of the tenth century, at the same time that the monastic movement expanded and prospered. The Benedictine monks constructed their monasteries in the Romanesque style, influencing the design of churches all over Europe.

The major design elements of the style are massive stone walls, a round arch, and vaulting to carry the roof. Walls were generally of rubble and concrete faced with brick or stone, and were sometimes stuccoed. Columns, built of ashlar masonry with a rubble core, were carved with decorative patterns.

In comparison with the long, low basilicas of the early Christian Church, Romanesque churches were lofty and boldly massed. In part, this change was due to advances in building techniques, but the development of the Romanesque style also reflected the evolving relationship between individual worshipers and their God. While earlier basilicas preserved a sensibility left over from the days of persecution under the Roman Empire, the Romanesque churches expressed a new attitude. As the Christian Church grew, church buildings became beautifully expressive of God's glory and grandeur.

Churches in England underwent a transformation similar to that of churches in western Europe following the Norman Conquest of 1066. The Normans' consolidation of their invasion was accompanied by a building boom in which virtually every church and abbey was rebuilt. It was this surge of new construction work that introduced the Romanesque style to the British Isles, and it is for this reason that the Romanesque style is called Norman in that part of the world.

Seen from the churchyard, St. Dunstan's Church in Canterbury,, England, exhibits the side tower brought to the British Isles by the Normans.

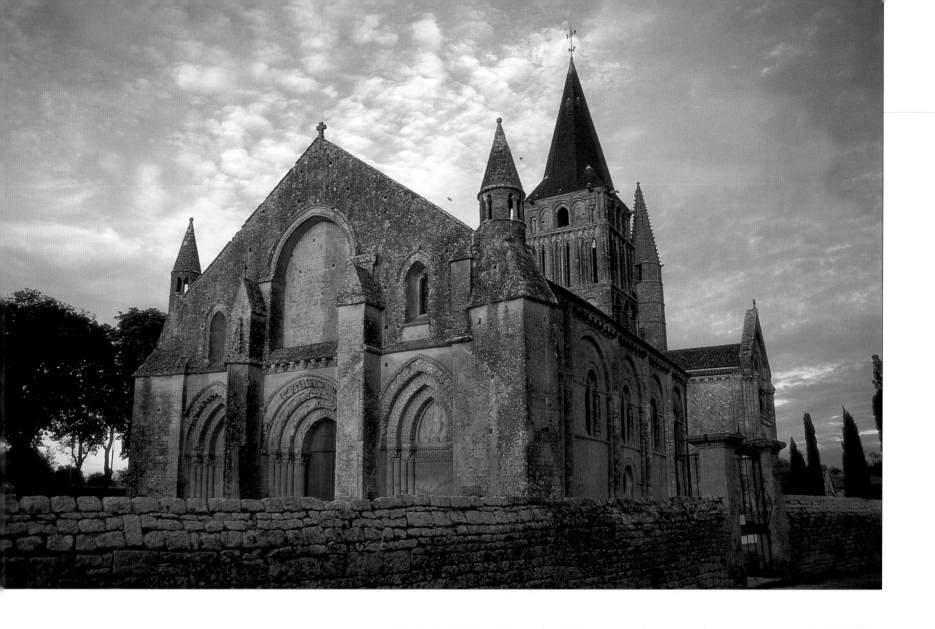

ABOVE: *Gradually, the decorative spirit of the Romanesque was extended to enrich church exteriors. In the twelfth century, portals were adorned with elaborate figures, decorative moldings, and sculpted tympana depicting saints and fabulous creatures, as in the entranceway at Aulnay-de-Saint-Onge, Poitou-Charentes region, France.* RIGHT: *In Romanesque architecture, the structure itself was carved, in contrast with Byzantine and early Christian churches, which were decorated with a veneer of marble or mosaic tile.*

Gothic Churches

The next major development in the evolution of church architecture was the introduction of the Gothic style. The aim of Gothic builders was to bring light and spaciousness into previously dark interiors by piercing the heavy walls with many decorative windows, allowing light to stream in. Instead of relying entirely on the side walls, the roof is supported by a system of ribbed, and pointed arches; this key innovation allowed for the increased openings in the side walls.

Like the Romanesque style, the Gothic became possible only because of technical developments in the builder's art. In particular, the introduction of the flying buttress and the pointed arch made it possible to greatly reduce the load placed on the external walls, which in turn allowed the walls to be made lighter, leaving much more space for windows.

Just as the introduction of the Romanesque style had expressed the

ABOVE: *Romanesque pilasters and the concentric carved tympana became elaborate works of art, as in this example from the Bordeaux region of France.*
OPPOSITE: *The groin vaulted ceiling in this church in Gloucestershire, England, demonstrates the light and exuberant synthesis of structure and decoration in Gothic architecture. The use of carved stone tracery reduces the weight of the ceiling.*

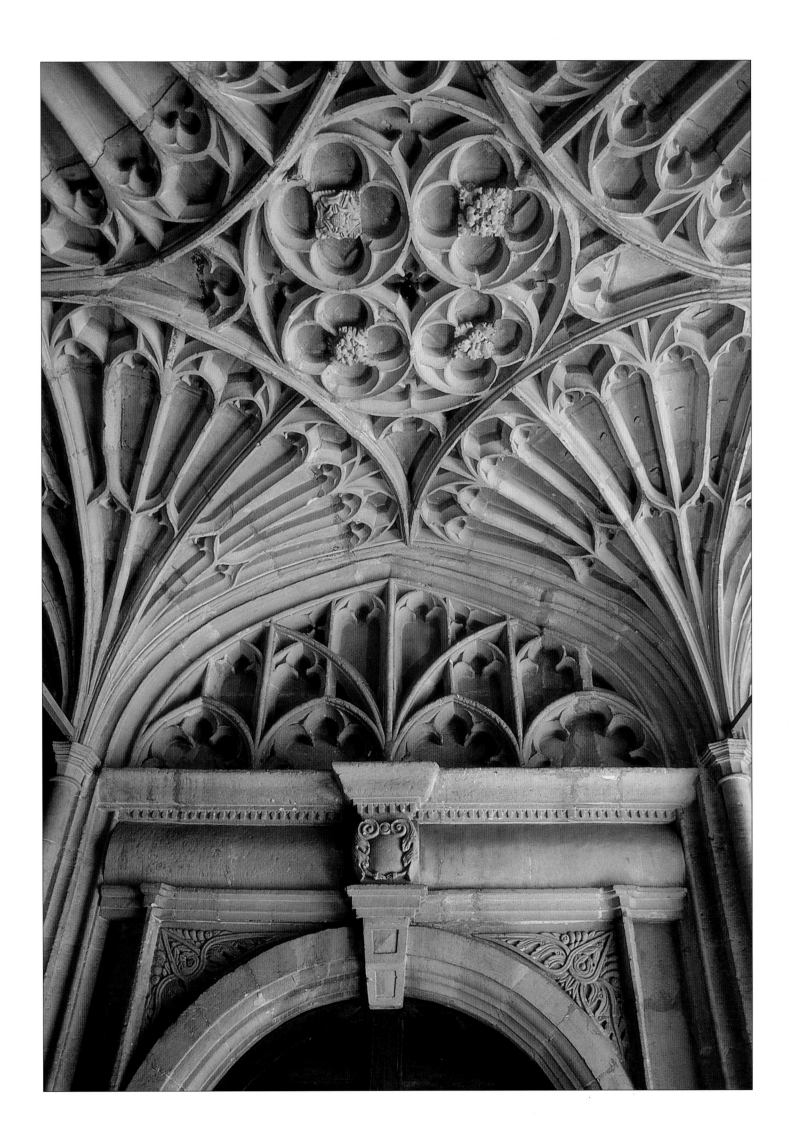

new strength and confidence of the Christian Church, so the Gothic style also reflected the changing attitudes of European society regarding God and the expression of religious faith. The new Gothic churches represented an emotional, aesthetic appreciation of God's glory.

During the High Middle Ages (c. 1050–1300), tens of thousands of parish churches were constructed across Europe. The churches were both Romanesque and Gothic in design, the edges between the two styles often blurred through years of rebuilding and alteration.

Today, of the thousands of small churches in Europe, most are of medieval origin.

The construction of these churches was often a community effort. As rural hamlets grew into more prosperous towns, churches were enlarged and made more elaborate in a reverent demonstration of gratitude and pride. Every church, even the most modest, meant the expenditure of some wealth. Even poor communities devoted considerable time and resources to the parish church, which remained the focus of a community's spiritual, social, and cultural life up until the Industrial Revolution.

This village church in Nerigan, in the Aquitaine region of France, was built and rebuilt between the twelfth and sixteenth centuries.

Renaissance and Baroque Churches

For almost a thousand years following the fall of Rome, the Christian Church controlled European intellectual and spiritual life. In the late fourteenth century, however, this began to change. Northern Italy boasted a bustling urban society based on flourishing industries and profitable commerce. Stimulated by the resulting tremendous economic growth, a revolutionary expansion of literary, artistic, and cultural life—the Renaissance—occurred in the city-states of Italy and began to spread northward.

While the church had instructed that life was in the end unimportant except as a passage to eternal life after death, Renaissance thinkers disagreed, believing that the purpose of life was to develop one's potential, and to explore and study all things in the earthly world. This new humanism found its way into the arts quickly, and church designs began to reflect the new philosophy. Renaissance churches were designed to be seen from the front, and they were based on the classical architec-

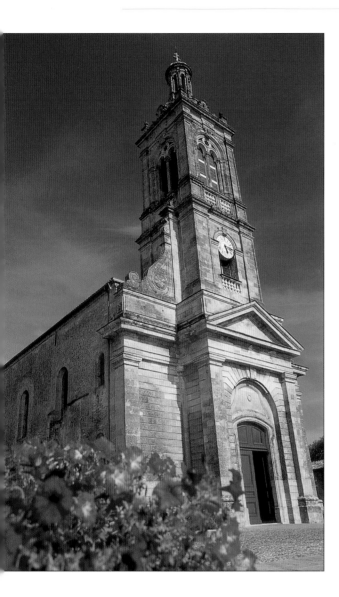

LEFT: *St. Estephe in France's Bordeaux region exhibits the Roman features—classical moldings and entablature, symmetrical design, and the element of stately and dignified repose—rediscovered and popularized by Renaissance architects. Note the ornamental brackets that join the lower façade to the bell tower.* BELOW: *The "Stiftskirche" or Stift Wilten Church (built 1661–1665) in Innsbruck, Austria, displays the exuberant theatricality of Baroque architecture. Designed by Christoph Gumpp, Jr., each floor is decorated with a different type of classical molding, and the semi-domed entrance bay extends to the top of the façade. The architecture is enhanced by bright yellow and salmon paint.*

ture of ancient Greece and Rome. Architects reintroduced the classical orders—Tuscan, Doric, Ionic, Corinthian, and Composite—but saw fit to use them in novel ways. Significantly, ornamentation in these churches was based on classical mythology rather than biblical motifs.

While Italian Renaissance churches expressly favored a horizontal design, typically forgoing towers and spires for a central dome,

St. Johannes Church, with its simple, onion-domed bell tower and churchyard cemetery. Grainau, Bavaria, Germany. Note the pitched roofs over each grave marker.

Renaissance-style churches in France and Northern Europe were more of an amalgamation of Gothic and Renaissance styles.

In sixteenth-century Italy, as the rules pertaining to Renaissance style hardened, a reaction set in among architects and artists who felt constrained by the prevailing ideal that all designs should be based on a classical precedent. A new style was born, even as architects in greater Europe were only beginning to employ the Renaissance style into their designs. The Baroque—from the French word for bizarre—took the initial Renaissance impulse of freedom of spirit and originality still further, attempting to break the rules and standards of classical proportion.

The Baroque is a decorative style almost theatrical in its use of applied ornament, and is inspired more by aesthetic than function. Columns are twisted, cornices and entablature are notched so that columns move through them, and walls are trimmed with top-heavy, scrolled cornices and outward leaning statues. Highly gilded curvilinear carved moldings and sculptures enliven crowded Baroque church interiors.

The Baroque style spread over Italy and into Spain and Portugal, where the Jesuit order adopted it and carried the style to Spain's far-flung colonies. In the seventeenth, eighteenth, and nineteenth centuries, Baroque churches were erected wherever Spanish explorers traveled or Jesuits preached. Soon there were more Baroque churches in the Americas than in all of Spain. The style came to Germany and Eastern Europe during the eighteenth century, and a few exquisite Baroque churches were built in the region.

Rural churches built or remodeled in the Renaissance or Baroque styles are relatively rare in much of Europe, as these styles were chiefly utilized for large town and city buildings. When employed in the country, they were most often used in building estates, palaces, and villas. Outside of Italy and Spain, however, it is still possible to find many country churches that exhibit Baroque-style interior decoration, typically curvilinear wood altars, screens, and choir rails elaborately carved by local craftsmen.

Village church with staged bell tower, Austria.

ABOVE: *Altar, Whitley Parish Church, Worcestershire, England.* RIGHT: *A flamboyant Baroque altarpiece, with elaborate classical moldings and ostentatious curvilinear carving, all covered in gold leaf. Ainhoa Church, Basque country, France.*

The Reformation

The Protestant Reformation was a reaction against what many considered to be the shameful spread of corruption and degeneracy within the Church. The illiteracy of many priests; the dissolute lives of some of the clergy, including some popes; the overt sale of religious offices and dispensations, and of indulgences, or pardons, for sins; all of this was intolerable to theologians and clergymen who took more seriously the dignity and responsibility of their positions. When the Church went so far as to offer indulgences for sale in order to pay for repairs to St. Peter's Church in Rome, it was the last straw, inspiring Martin Luther to post his ninety-five theses on the door of the Church of Wittenberg, Germany, in 1517. This "squabble among monks," as Pope Leo X arrogantly dismissed it, had an inflammatory effect that is hard to imagine today, and the resulting upheaval shook the entire Christian world to its core. Disputation and dissension led to wide-scale revolt in central Europe, particularly in the German territories. Churches all over Europe, particularly those with the most ornate decorations, were

ABOVE: A small, country church at Östergotana, Sweden. Note the entrance gate in the foreground, executed in stucco like the church. This gate and the walls of the churchyard indicate the entrance onto hallowed ground.

angrily defiled and destroyed by fanatical reformers.

In France, Germany, and elsewhere in Northern Europe, few churches were built during the Renaissance and the Reformation. With the decimation during the wars, and a new impulse toward colonization in the Americas, the local medieval parish church was still sufficient. The Protestant communities (which splintered into separate sects) made use of existing church buildings, and the now greatly reduced Catholic communities added Baroque work to replace interiors damaged by Protestant iconoclasts. The next great wave of church building—both Protestant and Catholic—was undertaken across the sea as the Age of Exploration and colonization carried Europeans to the new worlds, and with them, their ideas of church and community.

In consolidating their conquest of England, the Normans constructed or reconstructed virtually every church, cathedral, and castle. Chapel Royal of St. John on Tower Hill, London, built in 1078, was part of the Tower of London.

in the New World by Spanish colonists and missionaries.

In the nineteenth century, in a movement reminiscent of the Protestant Reformation (but far less violent), North American tastes and attitudes shifted again. Victorian clergymen began to consider it improper to worship Christ in a classically styled church, modeled after pagan temples. The Gothic style was resurrected as part of a deliberate search for genuinely Christian precedents in a movement called the Gothic Revival.

Meanwhile, in Europe, population increases led to the building of thousands of new churches, mostly in the developing urban areas, and the majority of these were in the Gothic Revival style. At the same time, many older churches were drastically remodeled by a generation of architectural purists who insisted that a church ought only to exhibit the style of its original construction, and that any later, discordant additions must be eliminated.

Eighteenth and Nineteenth Century Churches

In the eighteenth century, North America became the new locality of the humanist ideals that had fueled the Renaissance and the Reformation, with similar effects on church architecture. Classical styles were once more used for churches, but these churches were more often built out of wood than stone. The Baroque style was often employed

ABOVE: *The Royal Presidio Chapel, Monterey, California. The elegant Baroque portal façade has a single belltower attached to one side. The Presidio was the seat of secular government in each royal province in California.* OPPOSITE: *In the mid-nineteenth century, the Gothic Revival style spread from England to North America. Though constructed of wood, Christ Church in Ontario, Canada, exhibits pointed arch windows and portal, stained glass, and pinnacles and battlements on the upper stage of the bell tower—all derived from a Victorian view of medieval buildings.*

Chapter 2

Country Churches of the British Isles

Britain's history and culture are nowhere more apparent than in its rural churches. The variety of church buildings in Britain reflects an evolution of styles that stretches back more than a millennium.

Until the erosion of rural life and custom that began in the nineteenth century with the Industrial Revolution, the church was the most important place in English village society. During the High Middle Ages, some ten thousand parish churches dotted the English landscape, most of them in isolated hamlets, market and shire towns, and monastic settlements. In these churches, on Sundays, saints' days, and other holy days, entire villages and towns would gather for religious services and instruction. In a society where most people were illiterate, the church sermon was also an important source of news of events in the world outside the village. Along with weekly services, which were compulsory from the Middle Ages through 1690, virtually every meeting of a rural community took place in the church.

Early Influences

Christianity was established in Roman Britain by the third century A.D. Before the reign of the emperor Constantine, Christianity was merely one cult among many. But in 209, Albanus, a soldier, was martyred outside the city of Verulaminium, now called Saint Albans, and this event did a great deal to popularize the new religion in Britain. Almost 900 years later, in 1077, an abbey was established on the supposed site of the martyrdom, and it became a popular pilgrimage destination.

Irish Christianity drew its spiritual inspiration as much from contemplation of the natural world as from Roman liturgy. Small, stone chapel with round-arched portal, County Cork, Ireland.

In 410, the Roman legions withdrew from Britain, leaving the way open for successive invasions by pagan Germanic tribes—the Anglo-Saxons, the Jutes, and the Danes—in the fifth and sixth centuries. Apart from a few Roman towns—notably York, London, and Bath—Christianity was all but eliminated in England.

At the same time, however, Christianity continued to thrive in Ireland, Scotland, and Wales in its robust Celtic tradition. Advocating a direct, personal experience of Christ in nature and aestheticism, anarchistic and anti-hierarchical Celtic monks were energetic proselytizers who carried the gospel to the heathen regions of Europe.

In 597 missionaries led by Augustine and sent by Pope Gregory arrived in Britain and established a Benedictine monastery at Ethelbert's capital of Canterbury. The express mission of these monks was not only to spread the gospel but to strengthen the hold of the Roman Church, as opposed to the home-grown Celtic version of Christianity. As Christian evangelists spread out across the British countryside, they were encouraged to build churches at pre-Christian places of pagan worship. Patrick, Bishop of the Hebrides, commanded

the missionary Orlygus ". . . to build a church wherever he found a pagan stone circle or menhirs."

Little remains of the timber or masonry churches built by the early Celtic and Roman missionaries of the fifth and sixth centuries. As the Saxons built primarily in wood, most of their churches have disappeared as well.

The usual Anglo-Saxon church plan was generally quite plain. They frequently show a square-ended channel divided by a solid wall with a narrow arch. The church close — an area around a church building often bounded by a low wall — is another hallmark of English churches, and seems to have begun appearing in this period.

OPPOSITE: *St. Endoc's Church, at Trebetherick, Cornwall, fifteenth century, features a long, low nave, with side porch, and attached side tower.* RIGHT: *Kelso Abbey, built c. 1128, followed English and Continental design precedent, and has a cuneiform plan with vaulted, stone roofed, side aisles and timber framed roof in the nave. Roxburghshire, Borders, Scotland.*

The Norman Conquest

The conquest of England by William, Duke of Normandy, in 1066 ushered in the largest institutional building boom in English history until the urban growth of the Industrial Revolution. Castles and manor houses, cathedrals and local churches were rebuilt and elaborate new ones were constructed in an effort to consolidate Norman power.

The Normans were energetic builders, and they built new churches and cathedrals along the same stylistic lines as continental Romanesque designs. Many examples of Norman churches still stand today. They are characterized by a cruciform plan executed in thick stone walls, with high narrow windows, semicircular arches, and a tower at the western end. Cathedrals and larger parish churches built in the cruciform plan sometimes have a tower at the junction of nave and transepts. Some were given a rounded apsidal east end to the channel in the continental style, but most retained the traditional English square east end. These distinctive early Norman features are often

ABOVE: *Glastonbury Abbey, Somerset, England.* OPPOSITE: *Church at Stanton, Cotswolds, Gloucestershire, England.*

hidden by later additions such as aisles flanking the nave or clerestory.

Parish church roofs were typically open-framed in wood, as opposed to the stone vaulting favored on the Continent. English builders solved the problem of transmitting the weight of the roof to the side walls in different ways. Roof framing evolved from a simple tie-beam—two rafters whose ends are connected or tied by

a horizontal beam supporting the walls—to elaborate systems of trusses. The fourteenth-century hammer-beam structure featured a series of trusses without a cross tie. Such framing schemes, elegant and beautiful in themselves, were often carved and gilded, adding to their aesthetic effect.

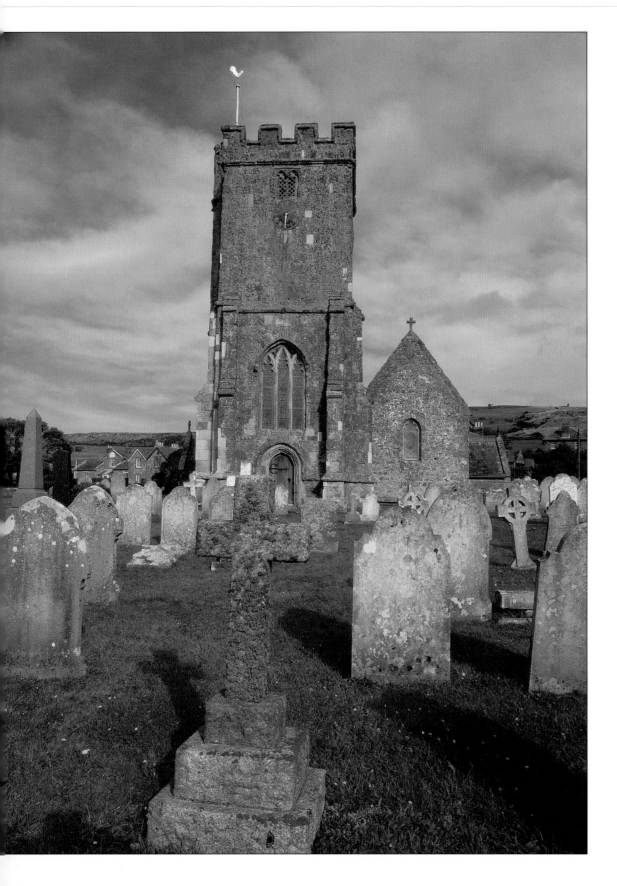

St. Andrew's Church, a twelfth-century Decorated Gothic church, exhibits the enlarged windows and window tracery, buttresses for wall support, and the battlemented parapet on the bell tower that are hallmarks of the style. Chale, Isle of Wight, England.

English Gothic

Beginning in the middle of the twelfth century, elements of Gothic style, including pointed arches and stone roof vaulting, began to be introduced in Britain. These elements initially appeared only in large cathedrals and churches, but later they began to show up in the smaller country churches. Three main phases of the Gothic style in Britain are generally distinguished by historians: Early English, c. 1150–1250; Decorated, c.1250–1380; and Perpendicular, c. 1350–1485.

Early English Gothic work features the compound column, in which the massive columns used in Romanesque or Norman construction are molded, lightening their visual effect. Narrow lancet windows and projecting buttresses for structural support are also typical of this style.

In Decorated Gothic construction, the thickness of church walls is reduced and the size of windows increased, thanks to a greater reliance on buttresses. This period also saw the increased carving of wall surfaces and the widespread use of window tracery, as well as the addition of battlemented parapets to church bell towers.

In the Perpendicular Gothic period windows are further enlarged and embellished with tracery, columns become more slender, and the hammer-beam roof frame becomes common.

Between 1420 and 1540, many new churches were constructed in the prosperous agricultural regions, the new construction funded by the affluent wool and cloth merchants of East Anglia and the Cotswolds. These so-called wool churches are still a notable feature of the farmland regions of England, and are particularly common in Norfolk, Suffolk, and the Cotswolds.

St. John the Baptist, Cirencester, was a Norman church, but it was embellished and enlarged in the Perpendicular Gothic style by wealthy wool merchants in the fourteenth and fifteenth centuries. The tower has three stories and is lavishly decorated with stone tracery and supported by buttresses. Stone pinnacles crown the tower buttresses and accentuate the verticality of the design.

OPPOSITE: *A modest, medieval, stone country church in Sapperton, Gloucestershire, England. Note the cruciform plan with central bell tower and polygonal stone steeple.* ABOVE: *The Christian heritage of Scotland dates to the monastical impulse of the Celtic Church. The corbeled dry-laid stone cells and round church towers of the early Middle Ages gave way to Norman monasteries and English and continental styles and design, though the Celtic element lived on in isolated country 'kirks.'*

The Reformation

In the sixteenth century, the Reformation fractured the Christian community in the British Isles. Links with Rome were broken, and the Catholic Church was replaced by one owing its allegiance to the English crown in England, Wales, and Ireland. In Scotland the Presbyterian Church dominated. Roman Catholicism survived in strength only in Ireland.

The deep and often violent struggles surrounding the nature of faith and the Church led to an era of widespread church destruction. Religious paintings and sculptures were viewed by Protestant reformers as offensive "popery." Oliver Cromwell's zealous soldiers "purified" many churches by removing, painting over, or destroying their artwork.

Renaissance and Gothic Revival

From the Reformation up until the nineteenth century, there was very little new church construction in Britain. The notable exception in this hiatus was the rebuilding of London following the fire of 1666. Sir Christopher Wren and his pupil Nicholas Hawksmoor designed magnificent city churches in the neoclassical Renaissance style, with columned porticoes, domes, and

From the dawn of Christianity through the late Middle Ages, churches did not have pews, though there might be benches for the old and infirm along the sides of the nave, giving rise to the expression, "the weak to the wall." Church interior, Camden, England.

Sanctuary, Gothic interior with choir seating decorated with crockets, Thirsk Church, England.

tiered bell towers. By the beginning of the nineteenth century, classical styles still had their exponents, but most of the new churches built in Victorian England harkened back to the Gothic style.

The Gothic Revival, which began in the late eighteenth century, was largely fueled by the popular literature of the day. Through the works of such celebrated writers as Victor Hugo and Sir Walter Scott, Britons who felt increasingly alienated by the rapid social and environmental changes brought about by the Industrial Revolution took comfort in dreams of a wonderfully romantic medieval past. Clergymen also argued that a Christian people should worship in a Christian building, not in one modeled on a pagan Greek or Roman temple, such as the Renaissance style produced. New churches were built, and older ones rebuilt, using irregular massing and flamboyant Gothic decoration. This often resulted in churches that were more exuberantly "Gothic" than anything built during the initial Gothic period of the Middle Ages.

In 1828 one million pounds was voted by Parliament to build 214 new churches, mostly for the exploding populations of London and other industrial towns. Of these, about 170 were built in the Gothic Revival style.

Scotland

While early Christian churches in Scotland are rare, there exists a rich heritage from the Celtic Church. Relic beehive monks' cells built of corbeled stone remain, and round towers dating from the tenth to the twelfth centuries survive in Tayside and Brechin. Celtic high crosses are found in conjunction with church buildings at Islay and Iona.

Scottish church architecture followed for the most part the English cruciform plan. The typical stylized parish church is Norman, or Romanesque, with round arches and elaborate carving on the capitals and moldings.

However, the Scottish Highlands, with its fiercely independent and isolated population, was also dotted with many small churches that were far less sophisticated in construction than even the simple Norman structures found in the Lowland and Hebridean towns.

Of these, the simplest were known as black kirks. These were plain rectangular stone naves with a west door, an east channel window, and a corbeled or thatched roof. A step up from the black kirks were the white kirks, with plastered and limewashed walls, which became the typical rural church in much of Scotland. These little country churches have long been dismissed as plain. The best of them, as described by twentieth century novelist Alastair Maclean, are "thoroughly and righteously plain, justifying themselves by apt proportions and . . . decency."

Church architecture came into its own with the independence of Scotland, won under the leadership of Robert Bruce at Bannockburn in 1314. Scottish ecclesiastical architecture began to follow French precedents, as both countries worked politically against England in the fourteenth century. But in 1560 John Knox (1502–1572), a disciple of the noted Protestant reformer

Gray Friars Kirk, Edinburgh, Scotland. This Gothic-style abbey church has vaulted side aisles and buttresses topped with pinnacles.

The basilican church plan was adaptable to a variety of locales and conditions. It could be built in different types of stone, brick, or wood, and could be roofed with stone, wood, or even thatch, like this example at Sustead, Norfolk, England.

John Calvin, united Scottish Protestants and established the Church of Scotland. The nobility forced the Catholic Mary Stuart to abdicate in favor of James I.

The major rift in the Scottish Church after the Reformation was the Disruption of 1843, in which Evangelical reformers found them-selves at odds with tradition-bound conservatives. Many dissenters quit the "auld kirk" and set up new, "free kirks." In a rhyme, these Dissenters contrasted their simple places of worship with the established parish churches, which they viewed as unresponsive to the spiritual needs of a dwindling congregation:

> *The Free Kirk,*
> *the wee Kirk,*
> *The Kirk without*
> *the steeple,*
> *The Auld Kirk, the*
> *cauld Kirk,*
> *The Kirk without*
> *the people.*

Ireland

Ireland was Christianized by Saint Patrick in the fifth century, but it had never been a part of the Roman Empire, and the Celtic Church developed along divergent lines. Irish worship differed from the Roman Church in several aspects, including a different date for Easter and different prayers during mass. Irish priests wore a distinct kind of tonsure, shaving the entire front of the head instead of only the top, as Roman priests did. The Irish were also contrary in naming their churches for living persons, and in immersing only once in the rite of baptism, compared to three times in the Roman sacrament. In addition, the Celtic Church was organized along strict monastic

lines, disregarding the European diocesan hierarchy.

The Irish gave their Christianity a particularly Hibernian slant, assimilating native pagan lore and fusing the new religion with older tradition. Missionaries and hermits drew their spiritual inspiration as much from the natural world as from books and the liturgy. The result was decidedly un-Roman— robust, passionate, and independent.

Glendalough monastery in Wicklow was founded by St. Kevin in the sixth century and retains early beehive huts, a modest stone church with round tower dating from the twelfth century, and a freestanding eleventh-century round tower. The tower has a door in the second story, and is said to have functioned as a place of refuge during raids. At one time, there were a hundred or more of these towers in Ireland and Scotland. Their purpose has puzzled antiquarians, some of whom have proposed a connection with a cult of phallic worship. But most agree that they were probably built as belfries as the Gaelic name—cloigtheach, meaning "bell tower"—suggests.

OPPOSITE: *Beneath Brandon Mountain, from where St. Brendan the Navigator is said to have seen the blessed isles of the West, Kilmalkedar Church is sited on the ruins of an earlier pagan settlement. Built in the Irish Romanesque style during the twelfth century, the stone church exhibits a decorated round arched portal, corner buttresses, and the remains of a stone cross in the gable peak.* ABOVE: *Beehive huts, Dingle Penninsula, Ireland. Built without mortar, these corbeled stone structures date from the sixth to eighth centuries. Irish monks adapted this prechristian building method for use as monastic cells.*

OPPOSITE: *Romanesque and Gothic architecture were brought to Ireland first by missionaries from continental Europe, and later by invading Normans.* ABOVE: *Saint Kevin founded the monastery at Glendalough in the sixth century, and it flourished as a center of art and learning in the two centuries after. His 'Kitchen,' or church, dates from the twelfth century. County Wicklow, Ireland.*

From the sixth to the ninth century, monasteries were the only settlements comparable to towns in Ireland, and villages typically grew up around them. Centers of art, culture, wealth, and learning, they were often ruled by abbots whose titles were handed down from father to son. Rejecting the Roman diocesan system, monasteries founded satellite settlements, and new monasteries gave their allegiance to the more dominant mother house.

Irish missionaries were also influential on the Continent, founding religious communities at Gall (Switzerland), Luxeuil (France), Bobbio (Italy), and Enternach (Germany) by 1036. The Germans even have a term, Schottenkirche, for churches founded by peripatetic twelfth-century Irishmen. By the eleventh century, however, the Church of Rome had firmly established its supremacy throughout Western Europe.

In 1169 Leinster chieftain Dermot MacMurrough sought military aid against neighboring chieftains from Henry II. The Normans came in force. They stayed and over time subdued the fragmented Irish kingdoms. As everywhere else in the British Isles, Norman architecture was highly influential in Ireland.

During the Reformation, the majority of Irish people remained Catholic. Sixteenth-century attempts by Henry VIII, Mary Tudor, and Elizabeth I to dissolve monasteries and establish the Church of England met with hostility and widespread resistance. Beginning in 1609, however, the Plantation of Ulster colonized Ireland with large numbers of English and Scottish Protestants. In 1578 St. Patrick's Church of Newry, Ulster, the first Protestant Church in Ireland, was built. Anglo-Irish satirist Jonathan Swift, himself an Anglican minister, caustically remarked of the town, "High church, low steeple, dirty town, proud people."

The Irish seized the opportunity to rebel during the English civil war, but were brutally conquered and returned to the Commonwealth by Oliver Cromwell. Catholic Irish were slaughtered, priests hanged, and churches and monasteries burned and plundered. Under the harsh Penal Laws of 1695, Catholics were excluded from government and economically disadvantaged. All Catholic priests were banned except for a single pastor at each church if he took an oath of allegiance to the Crown. Catholic "hedge" priests celebrated the mass in secret.

The Great Famine of 1845 killed a million Irish people, and forced more than a million others to leave the country. Warfare and religious strife, along with economic hardship and chronic emigration, have left many of Ireland's historic country churches as beautiful, moving ruins testifying to the island's turbulent history. But the piety of the Irish people has also made Ireland one of the strongest bastions of rural parish community life.

OPPOSITE: *The characteristic feature of Celtic Christian monasticism is the round tower, often more than ninety feet (27.4m) high with a second story entrance reached by ladder, and capped with a conical roof. Once thought to have been places of retreat during Viking raids, they are now believed to have served as belfries. Glendalough, County Wicklow, Ireland.*

Chapter 3

Country Churches
of Western Europe

One can still glimpse the timeless patterns of village life in the small community churches of western Europe. In Italy and France, for example, a stop at the church or cemetery, a quick confession, and a genuflection in front of the altar are still daily tasks for large sections of the population. To enter the cool shadows of any one of the thousands of old country churches is to find that—across centuries marked by political, economic, and social change, the Reformation, the Industrial Revolution, and two world wars—the Christian life of medieval Europe survives relatively unchanged. These simple, unpretentious churches of stone and timber stand today as testimony to the vitality, creativity, and faith of generations of country people.

Early Churches

Little remains of the earliest Christian churches in continental western Europe. In Italy, early house and hall churches were rebuilt as monumental ecclesiastical buildings during the reigns of Constantine and his successors up to Justinian. The earliest churches in Gaul and Iberia were simple stone or timber halls with square or rectangular naves and wood framed roofs. Many of these early buildings have been uncovered by archaeologists on the sites of later great churches, such as those at Bonn, Cologne, and St. Maurice d'Agaune.

As the Roman Empire began to crumble in the fourth and fifth centuries, western Europe was invaded by successive waves of migratory tribes from the east, including the Vandals,

Regardless of the arrangement, building materials, and style, an unpretentious nave, bell tower, and yard are still the timeless rudiments of community and spiritual inspiration in Western Europe. The Haly Church in the Dolomite mountains.

The Romanesque church at Torla, in Aragon, in the Pyrenees Mountains of Northern Spain, is a complex and organic assembly of rectangular and polygonal shapes, accented by small windows. The color and texture of the masonry walls and the shallow, tiled roofs give the structure a sense of coherence.

Visigoths, and Franks. These peoples were converted to Christianity, and by the end of the eighth century the Franks had emerged as the dominant political force in Europe. During this time of convulsion and upheaval, known as the Pre-Carolingian period, the Roman Church acted to fill the power vacuum that was left all across the continent by the removal of Roman Imperial authority.

Not many churches survive in continental Europe from this period. A few exist in Spain, having been built by the Visigoths, who accepted Christianity in 587 and were conquered by the Moslems in 711. The buildings are small, single-naved, without aisles, and are built in carefully hewn and fitted stone. Some of these churches are built in the cruciform plan. In Northern Europe there were also single-nave churches that were built in wood, of which only anecdotal evidence survives.

The Carolingian Renaissance and the Romanesque Explosion

When the Frankish king Charlemagne was crowned Emperor on Christmas day in 800, it marked the beginning of what is known as the Carolingian Renaissance. Charlemagne gathered learned clergymen to his palace school at Aachen, with the aim of creating an educated clergy capable of spreading the Christian faith. He organized missions to convert the Saxons, which was accomplished, finally, with fire and sword. He also sponsored missions to the Danes. He attempted to revive Roman culture in Northern Europe, and introduced the rudiments of Byzantine architecture—semicircular arches for windows, doors, and arcades, barrel vaulting for interior support, and massive walls and piers to support the outward force of the arches—which became the Romanesque style. The earliest Romanesque churches of France and Germany date from this period.

After Charlemagne's death, his kingdom fragmented quickly under

The Benedictine Church of St. Foy stands on the pilgrimage route to Santiago de Compostela. Built in 1055 to hold the remains of the Saint, it was greatly expanded to handle the growing number of pilgrims in 1200. An aisled transept, additional chapels, and ambulatory were added to its original basilica design. Conques, France.

Vaulted stone crypts were often constructed below the body of the church, supporting the building and often containing a chapel, relics, and tombs where deceased nobles, merchants, and clergymen were interred. This crypt supplies a foundation for the eleventh-century Romanesque church at Leyre Monastery, at the village of Vesa, Navarra, Spain.

the pressures of dynastic struggle and Viking raids.

The civil and administrative organization of the Church took shape during the Carolingian period The diocesan hierarchy in which bishops oversaw a diocese made up of parishes—each with its own pastor—prevailed in Europe through the Middle Ages until the Reformation. Older bishops' sees in Italy and southern France were small, having been created for early congregations. However, in regions that were not converted until the eighth and ninth centuries, dioceses might cover widespread areas. The spiritual care of the faithful in the few towns and wider countryside was in the hands of the parish priest. During this time, country churches sprang up all across western Europe.

The eleventh century witnessed the slow return of political stability to western Europe. Foreign invasions gradually declined and domestic disorders subsided. Germanic and Scandinavian peoples who had troubled the Christian world were by this time

This church features a well-buttressed polygonal apse and square side tower. Alsace, France.

absorbed into the Christian culture themselves. Political order and security provided the foundations for a general economic recovery through increased trade and commerce. The revival of the Church manifested itself in a flowering of popular piety, expressed in the building of great cathedrals and churches, and in the rebuilding of timber churches in stone, in the Romanesque style.

A Cluniac monk, Raoul Glaber, wrote of the early years of the eleventh century: "Christians competed with one another in renewing their churches in a more elegant style. It was as if the world . . . , throwing off the old, was everywhere clothing itself in a white robe of churches. Then the faithful improved almost all the cathedrals, as well as monasteries dedicated to various saints, and even the little village chapels."

The earliest Romanesque churches were built in southern France, Spain, and northern Italy.

The Romanesque style was interpreted differently in the various regions of Europe, based on local tradition, environment, and available materials. Romanesque churches in Italy have shallow, tiled roofs and small windows to keep out the harsh sunlight, while those built in Germany have steeply pitched roofs to prevent the accumulation of snow, and wider windows to let in as much light as possible. German Romanesque churches often have a square plan, double channel, and square or polygonal towers, sometimes topped with a distinctive helmed roof. In Belgium, the tenth-century church at Invelles, and the church at Liège, which was built in the twelfth and thirteenth centuries, are notable examples of Romanesque design, as is the church at Maastricht in Holland.

At the local parish level, most churches were much less ambitious than cathedrals and monastery churches. However, they do show a marked increase in ornament. Also, steeples began to appear at the west ends of churches or over the crossing in a cruciform plan. An increase in saints' cults frequently necessitated the addition of extra chapels within, or attached to, local churches. The rood screen—a wooden cross and screen dividing the nave from the choir—began to appear in this period.

By 1215 the parish system was firmly entrenched in western Europe, to the extent that the Lateran Council of Rome was able to take it for granted that every soul had a parish when it commanded that all Christians make confession to their pastor at least once a year.

The results of several renovations are evident in St. Saturnin les Apt. The nave and chancel are built of different materials, and on the near wall, a window has been closed in. Provence, France.

Gothic Churches

Gothic architecture originated in France and predominated there from about 1150 until the sixteenth century. The first Gothic church was St. Denis, which replaced the old Carolingian Romanesque church on a site on the outskirts of Paris in 1144. Architectural innovations such as the ribbed vault, stained-glass windows, pointed-arch windows, and the flying buttress were known before this time. At St. Denis, however, these new techniques made possible an extraordinary interior light, perhaps difficult to appreciate in an age when electricity allows us to take indoor lighting for granted. The flood of light through wall-sized stained-glass windows astounded King Louis VII and the dignitaries, bishops, and townspeople that had gathered for the consecration.

The Gothic rebuilding of Europe was an extraordinary achievement. Between 1180 and 1270 in France

A subterranean church hewn out of the rock face by Benedictine monks between the ninth and twelfth centuries, this monolithic religious structure is a testament to the spiritual faith and determination that infused the Middle Ages. The carved doorway dates from the fourteenth century. Town of St. Emilion, Aquitaine, France.

alone, tens of thousands of parish churches were constructed, along with some eighty cathedrals and perhaps five hundred monastery churches, in a country of about eighteen million people. French monks introduced the Gothic style to Spain in the early twelfth century. In both Italy and Germany, the Romanesque style of church building was very strong, and the Gothic style emerged late. The classical and Romanesque traditions had emphasized the horizontal plane of a building, and the soaring verticality that was the hallmark of Gothic design was not influential in either country.

In Belgium, the Gothic style also arrived late, coinciding with the thirteenth- and fourteenth-century growth of prosperity in this region based on cloth manufacture and commerce. Much of the new construction in this region is civic rather than religious. In Holland, though Gothic influences may be seen, churches, built of brick with steep roofs, remained fairly plain.

A simple hall church with a nave and chancel of fieldstone, with dressed stone quoins and arches. The front portico and bell tower are of wood. Dale Stone Church, Village Luster, Breheimen, Norway.

The Renaissance

Architects during the Renaissance built churches on a centralized plan, usually preferring circular, polygonal, and Greek cross forms rather than the longer Latin cross prevalent in Romanesque and Gothic designs. Taking its cue from classical architectural forms, Renaissance designs emphasized symmetry. Renaissance buildings were typically freestanding, their centers covered by a dome. Most smaller churches were built in a truncated Greek cross style, in which four apses act as the arms, as opposed to the earlier styles in which a central nave had two flanking transepts. The altar space in the new churches was located in the eastern apse, sometimes accentuated by a round design.

Renaissance architects championed the location of a central altar beneath the dome as most authentically classical. However, the Church hierarchy resisted this, as it was considered an Eastern practice. In the Western church the celebration of mass was viewed from in front of the altar, and the Church fathers would not allow mass "in the round."

ABOVE: *The Renaissance emphasis on symmetry is evident in this church in Finland.* OPPOSITE: *This small town church on the Côte D'Azur is typical of the churches of coastal Provence.*

ABOVE: *Silhouetted against the Agean Sea, this open bell tower rises dramatically above a church on the Greek Island of Thera.* OPPOSITE: *A small whitewashed church in Mykonos, Greece incorporates such Byzantine elements as a central dome.*

The Reformation

The Protestant Reformation caused widespread destruction of church and religious artwork in France and Northern Europe, in Switzerland, and in large sections of Germany and Austria. The Church was the most important and all-embracing institution of the time, the very bedrock of western European culture and society for centuries past. As theological arguments—some of them hair-splitting debates over obscure doctrinal details, others genuinely substantial disagreements over widely recognized issues—became common and public, the resulting crisis had a palpable impact on every Christian in Europe. In Catholic churches everywhere, Protestant reformers were viciously denounced from the Sunday pulpit. At Protestant services, the Catholic church was similarly reviled.

The turmoil of the Reformation did not encourage church building.

Sogne Fjord, in western Norway, is the site of the world's oldest stave (or timber church, built c. 1130-1150.

The interior of St. Olaf Church in rural Sweden features an elaborate vaulted ceiling above the gilded altar. Both are typical of medieval architecture.

After clearing away the signs of popery, Protestant groups that took over local Catholic churches added galleries so that people could sit to better turn their attention to sermons, and pulpits from which to preach and be heard. Catholics, too, had little need for new churches, although during the Counter-Reformation, Jesuit groups made efforts to create a system of large churches to attract crowds in an attempt to counter the spread of Protestantism. Further, many church interiors that had been stripped or dismantled by Iconoclasts were replaced or refurbished in the Baroque style.

As Protestantism fragmented, small sects adopted houses and other structures as meeting places, much as their early Christian predecessors had done centuries earlier.

However, as the age of religious warfare came to a close in Europe in the eighteenth century, secure middle- and upper-class Protestants began to desire more elaborate churches. Catholics, too, followed a new impulse in church construction. But although many new churches were constructed, neither group built anything on the scale of the churches constructed during the Middle Ages.

The Age of Enlightenment and the Modern Age

Following the end of the Reformation's turmoil, the seventeenth and eighteenth centuries saw a general growth of humanism and secularism. Rapid advances in the sciences and mathematics led to a widespread belief in the capacity of human reason to penetrate and understand all the mysteries of nature.

Such a shift in attitude furthered a trend begun by the Reformation, which was to severely weaken the influence of the church in the secular spheres of politics and economics. Despite this, however, most Christians, whether Catholic or Protestant, retained a great deal of piety in their everyday lives. This piety was most fully expressed in the way small communities throughout Europe invested large amounts of money in their local churches. A notable example of this can be found in the parish closes, grand sculptural monuments depicting Christ's passion. These were erected over periods of as long as two hundred years in rural hamlets in Brittany during the sixteenth to eighteenth centuries, when the region had few urban centers but many prosperous rural settlements. Acute rivalries existed between neighboring villages, and these rivalries fueled the construction of many splendid closes.

In the past two centuries, the warfare and turmoil that scarred Europe involved the destruction of many rural churches and other sacred buildings. In certain cases, such as during the French Revolution, the Church was deliberately targeted, and many churches were looted or destroyed. Another factor in the devastation of rural churches dating back to the beginning of the Industrial Revolution has been the ongoing enormous shift in population from the country to the cities, draining rural parish congregations and leaving many churches

Baroque chancel, church interior, Vianden, Luxembourg. In rural areas, the Baroque is chiefly a style of remodeled interiors of medieval churches. This example demonstrates the theatrical nature of the style and what a single altar piece placed in a jewel-like setting can achieve.

While the onion dome may be an Islamic or Byzantine innovation, its ability to shed rain and snow led to its employment in Bavarian churches. The lighted Christmas tree, also a German tradition, casts a warm glow on this charming Bavarian chapel. Note the paintings on the façade, depicting Christ's crucifixion.

underused, underfunded, and, in some cases, simply abandoned.

In light of these many pressures, it is remarkable that in so many of the small parish churches of western Europe one may still discover the timeless traditions of family, community, and faith of which the buildings themselves are but a humble legacy.

Chapter 4

Country Churches of Eastern Europe

The emperor Constantine, who reigned from 306 to 337 A.D., tried to maintain the unity of the Roman Empire, moving the capital from Rome to Constantinople. As a result of this, while imperial authority eroded in the West during the fifth century, the political and social structures of Eastern Europe preserved the forms and traditions of the old Roman Empire at Constantinople, and even called themselves Romans. As the West declined into the Middle Ages, the East maintained a high standard of living. More important was the role of Byzantium as preserver of the wisdom of the ancient world. As Western Europe struggled to forge a new kind of society, the eastern empire protected the intellectual heritage of Greek and Roman civilization.

The Division of the Church

The position of the church in society differed considerably in the Byzantine East from what it was in the West. Constantine had used the Church to unify the Empire, but Germanic invasions made this unity more and more difficult to maintain. In the East, the emperor's jurisdiction over the church remained complete, while in the West, the church managed to fill the vacuum left by the decay of Roman imperial authority, with priests and bishops becoming deeply involved in social and political affairs. Eastern Church leaders were products of a more isolated, monastic spiritual life. Nevertheless, Roman popes, selected by the clergy of Rome, still informed the Emperors of Constantinople of their elections. Roman popes considered

The Eastern Church distinguished itself from its Western counterpart with unique architectual stuylee, as evidenced by this bright blue Bulgarian village church.

themselves bishops of the entire Roman Empire, but this soon became an empty claim.

As Islam spread across the Mediterranean in the seventh and eighth centuries, the two Churches were further divided. In 1054 theological disputes led the bishop of Rome and the Patriarch of Constantinople to excommunicate each other, creating a split between the Roman Catholic and Greek Orthodox churches that continues to this day. Differences between them deepened as the Eastern Church became more directly influenced by the incursions of other cultures from the East, including those of the Arabs, Turks, and Slavs.

In the fifteenth century, the Byzantine empire, by this time a weakened shell of its former self, collapsed with the fall of Constantinople to the Turks in 1453. Since that time, the various sects within the Eastern Church — Russian and Greek Orthodox, Balkan, and Armenian — have preserved early Christian forms and practices with great tenacity.

ABOVE: *A shallow dome sits on a whitewashed polygonal drum over the sanctuary of a village church at Ios. Note the open belfry formed by extending the parapet of the front façade. Santorini Island, Greece.*
OPPOSITE: *St. Basil's Cathedral, built by Tzar Ivan the Terrible from 1555 to 1560, is considered the preeminent symbol of spiritual Russia. The plan represents a star from which radiate eight chapels, each crowned with an onion-domed tower of contrasting height, shape, and decoration.*

ABOVE: *In the Eastern Church, where sculpture was considered idolatrous, painted icons, frescoes, and mosaic murals were the main decorative feature. Greek and Russian Orthodox communities have continued to build their churches in traditional style, and as immigrants have taken this religious and architectural ideal around the world. Holy Virgin Cathedral, San Francisco, California.* RIGHT: *Alexander Nevsky Church, Copenhagen, Denmark. Also called the Russian Church, it is dedicated to the Russian national hero who fought the Mongols.*

Eastern Church Architecture

Byzantine church architecture, as it developed by the fifth century, features round arched buildings constructed on a Greek cross plan, with the crossing covered by a domed roof. To support a dome without overly massive walls, Byzantine builders placed stone brackets, called pendentives, at the corners of each bay, creating a circular base for the dome. This made the engineering of the transition from dome to side walls straightforward. The scheme was repeated throughout the territories that fell under Byzantine rule and culture.

In the Eastern Church, sculpture was seen as idolatrous. Painted icons and mosaic murals, some spanning the entire interior of a church dome, were the main decorative features to be found in Byzantine churches. Typically, Christ as the Pantocrator—"Ruler of All Things"—is painted in the dome, Mary in the apse, and the patron saint and other saints—St. Michael, St. Nicholas, and St. George—on the iconostasis. A significant feature

A magnificent polychrome composition built in 1911, less than a decade before the Russian Revolution that led to a ban on religion and the seizure and closing of churches and religious institutions. Andrei Zenkov Cathedral, Alma-Ata, Kazakhstan.

of every Eastern Church, the iconostasis is a screen that divides the altar and sanctuary from the rest of the church. A pair of doors in the center are kept closed until communion.

The question of the representation of God and the saints had long been a troublesome one in the Eastern Church. One effect of the Jewish tradition on Christianity was

Crosses mark graves outside a Byzantine-style church in Canada. Holy Trinity Russian-Greek Orthodox Church, Smokey Lake, Alberta.

to spread the idea that the portrayal of religious subjects was idolatrous. In 726 the church was divided between iconoclasts, who wished to remove representational artwork, and iconodules, who wished to keep them. The iconodules eventually won out, thus cementing the place of the icon in the Eastern Church.

The Byzantine style is predominant in Eastern Europe for parish church building, even though the Catholic and Lutheran Churches gained adherents during the sixteenth century in Poland, Hungary, and the Baltic regions. Baroque altars dating from the seventeenth century may be found in some considerably older Byzantine churches. A tradition of timber church construction survives in Eastern Europe, dating from the seventeenth and eighteenth centuries. Parishes in the northern parts of Eastern Europe tend to be quite spread out, therefore many country churches feature a *soboty* (Polish for "Saturday"), which is a wooden roofed porch where families who had traveled long distances could sleep on Saturday evening, so as to be present for Sunday mass.

The Carpathian Mountain region holds a multitude of delightful Catholic, Greek, and Russian Orthodox wood churches. The small wooden church in Sekowa, for example, is one of the most beautiful examples of timber architecture in Poland. The main part of the building dates to the 1520s, which has a bell tower and a soboty. The soboty, added in the seventeenth century, looks like a verandah extending around the church, .

The wooden churches of Russia are particularly evocative, with their octagonal forms, wraparound porches, apron roofs, and onion domes. Sadly, most of these architectural masterpieces have fallen to fire and war. Before the Revolution, many hundreds had existed; the few surviving examples date from the eighteenth century.

Country parishes in Eastern Europe are often spread out. Many of the traditional country churches feature a soboty, a wrap-around porch, or extended eaves where the congregation could shelter on Saturday night, to be at Sunday service. Hobbitza Village, Romania.

Communist Rule and the Eastern Church

The churches of Eastern Europe had difficult times during the warfare and political turmoil of the past century. Religion was strictly controlled under Communist rule, which was officially atheistic. Religious instruction, services, and the ordination of priests were banned and many churches were seized for government use.

The Russian Orthodox Church survived by making an uneasy truce. Political matters were avoided and religious instruction to the young limited. During World War II, Joseph Stalin allowed some churches to be opened so Russians could pray for victory, understanding the importance of the Orthodox Church to the Russian soul. Under Communist rule, rural churches were used as stables, warehouses, schools, and daycare centers, or simply ignored. With the demise of the Soviet Union, the Church has again become a magnet for spiritual and nationalist sentiment in Eastern Europe.

ABOVE: *Many monasteries in the seventeenth and eighteenth centuries had new buildings constructed within their walls. Following the artistic influence of Moscow, they typically built in the Baroque style. New Virgin Monastery, Russia.* OPPOSITE: *Greek cross in plan, with a high nave, polygonal apse and drum, the fourteenth-century Church of St. Jovan Bogoslou also exhibits semicircular arches framing the drum windows to form a rippling eaves pattern. Ourid, former Yugoslavia.*

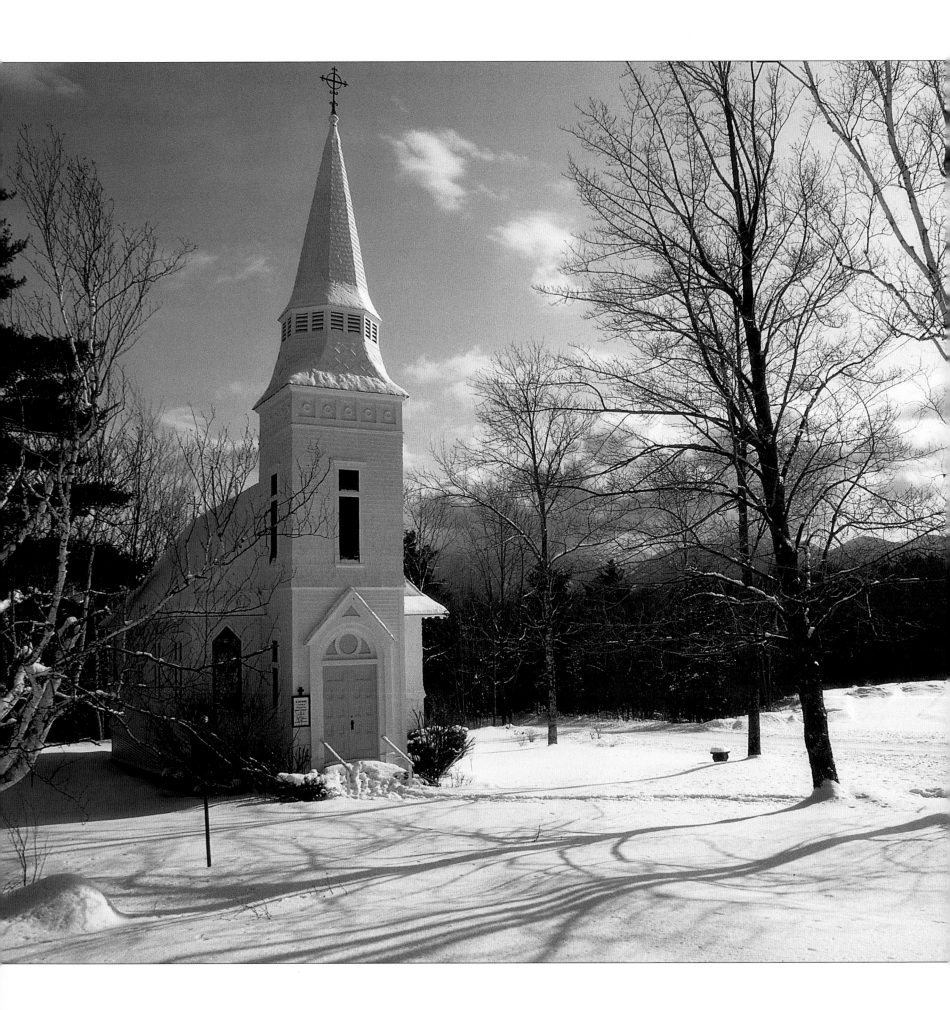

Chapter 5

Country Churches of North America

Throughout North America's colonial period, the church or meetinghouse was the most important structure in any community. The houses of worship that still stand from early communities testify to the strength and variety of religious practice in the New World.

The Southwest

The Spanish Colonial churches of the American Southwest were built of sun-dried adobe, a material and method long used by Native Americans of the region. Limestone, rubble stone, and baked brick were also employed, but these were often covered with stucco or adobe and smoothed, creating broad, starkly plain wall areas.

The front façade of a Southwestern adobe church is often emphasized by a belfry, a shaped gable, and an ornate portal. The size of a church, whether a mission or a parish house, was to a great extent limited by the length of the timbers available to support the roof. Typically, door and window openings are small and limited, partly for defense but also to keep out the sun.

The simplest of the Southwestern churches are in New Mexico, which was the far northern frontier of New Spain, and which experienced the secularization of its missions in the late eighteenth and early nineteenth centuries, in part because of a dearth of trained clergy in the area. Many village churches were run by nonordained curates and by local societies such as the Penitentes. The churches reflect the artistic skills of native laborers and the evolving folk

Snow blankets the ground outside a quaint country church in rural New Hampshire.

ABOVE: *The native construction material of the Southwest was adobe—mud mixed with straw, molded and baked by the sun into brick. Once walls were raised, they were covered with a finish of clay. The courtyard entrance to the Chapel of Our Lady of Guadeloupe in Albuquerque, New Mexico, demonstrates the plastic, organic form that adobe architecture takes.* OPPOSITE: *Altar bedecked with saints' images, locally carved rail, and devotional candle table testify to the continuing importance of religious faith in this community. Interior of Santo Niño Church, c. 1850-1860, Chimayo, New Mexico.*

tradition of the first generations of native-born Hispanics. Except for the portal, wood-paneled doors, and carved rails, there is little or no outside decoration. The simple technique of roof framing results in log roof timbers, called vegas, extending out through the side walls.

California mission churches were typically embellished with pilasters, pediments, and moldings. The twenty-one Franciscan missions established along the coast of California in the late eighteenth and early nineteenth centuries were constructed with Indian labor, but show the work of sophisticated Mexican craftsmen in their mix of Renaissance and Baroque styling. The mission churches of Texas and Arizona are grander and more ornate still, featuring sophisticated Baroque portals.

In New Mexico, church exteriors are frequently embellished with folk murals, carved wooden images of saints, and *reredos*, or altar screens. Church interiors of the other regions are decorated with Baroque altar pieces and gilded woodwork.

LEFT: *Geographic isolation and a strong tra- dition of local craft and devotional artistry result in unpretentious and forthright solu- tions to decoration and adornment. Weathered, domed belfry of a whitewashed church, Ysidro, New Mexico.* ABOVE: *A sunlit window opening reveals the thick walls used in adobe construction. Adobe is a product of the com- bined building traditions of Moorish and Catholic Spain and Pueblo Indian building. Thick walls and small window openings modi- fy extremes of temperature in the interiors. Santo Niño Chapel.* OPPOSITE: *An adobe church of simple solids and voids with side walls forming the twin bell towers of the façade. The recessed entranceway features a balcony supported by scrolled posts, and a stepped parapet. The Church at Taos Peublo, New Mexico.*

The Hawaiian Islands

Prior to the island chain's discovery by Western explorers in 1778, Hawaiian tribal worship was conducted at natural sites and sacred precincts. Protestant missionaries constructed the first church, little more than a thatch-roofed hut, in 1820. Northern European and American building styles were favored, but churches incorporated local environmental features. One of the most notable surviving early religious structures is Kawaiahao Church, Honolulu. This church built in 1842 in the then-popular Gothic Revival style, was constructed of coral shaped into blocks. It has a crennelated square bell tower, and a massive Doric portico.

ABOVE: *The interior of the pointed arched vault at St. Benedict Church, Kona, Hawaii, is elaborately painted in a tropical foliate motif.* OPPOSITE: *This diminutive wood-framed Catholic Church is sited on the beach at Kona. St. Peter's Church, Kona, Hawaii.*

The Eastern United States

In the English colonies, country churches were built of different materials, depending on the specific region. In the South, churches were often built of brick; in the Atlantic region, fieldstone is the preferred material; and in New England churches are usually timber-framed and sheathed with clapboard.

The basic Congregational meeting-house was large enough to hold the entire community, roughly square in plan, and fitted with boxed pews. The pulpit was opposite the door and might have a pulpit window for light.

Puritan doctrine prescribed that the meetinghouse not be decorated. Such simplicity has come to be much appreciated, valued for its pleasing austerity.

Native-born Yankees who resettled in northern New England beginning in the 1760s were secure in their religious freedom, and were less attached to this strict lack of ornamentation than were their Puritan forebears. By the time of the American Revolution, robust Georgian-style ornament—pedimented entrances and boldly worked cornices and window hoods—had become popular. In the South and mid-Atlantic regions, congregations built simple, refined Georgian churches, employing

embellishments such as classical moldings and corner quoins.

Following the American Revolution, the church form designed for the London suburbs by Christopher Wren was used in numerous new communities throughout the new nation, with hundreds of regional variations. The form consisted of the basic basilica style with a classical portico and steepled belfry. Georgian molding was refined and lightened into a style now called Federal, after the Federal era in United States history. Federal-style churches were built wherever New Englanders settled, in New York State, the Ohio Valley, and in the Midwest.

Classical ornament in the Federal style is elegant and slender. Steeples are divided into stages, and the most elaborate of them change from square at the base to polygonal and open stages, graduating to the pointed steeple. The Federal style defines the quintessential New England village church, though it is found throughout the United States.

ABOVE: *Unadorned, heavy timber framed, clapboard clad German Lutheran Church, with stairway in entrance block. Constructed in 1772 in Maine, this plain building evidences the simple form of worship European Protestants fought for and carried with them to the New World.* OPPOSITE: *The interior features include austere boxed pews and matching gallery, as well as a pulpit and pulpit window.*

ABOVE: *Late nineteenth-century wood-framed church with molded window lintels with brackets, corner boards, and closed pediment on the front gable. Note the louvered roof dormers in the steeple. The side bay entrance of this modest church is unusual. Sugarhill, New Hampshire.* RIGHT: *The ornate Federal period belfry may have been inspired by Asher Benjamin's handbook "The Country Builder's Assistant," and is a fine display of the vernacular carpenter's craft. In North America, wood became the preeminent building material. Castine, Maine.* OPPOSITE PAGE: *Modified by environment, community need, and personal whim, Federal-style churches were erected wherever New Englanders settled. Small white churches became the quintessential image of New England—and eventually American—community life.*

The popularity of the Greek Revival style reflected American admiration of the contemporary Greek War of Independence during the early nineteenth century, as well as the young nation's desire to honor what is considered to be the cradle of democracy. Swedenborgian Church, Bath, Maine.

Between 1825 and the American Civil War, the United States saw a national church building boom driven by vigorous migration and settlement, as well as agitation in the religious community. In this period American churches fragmented, and even well-settled townspeople who had shared a united church for years found themselves erecting separate buildings. Substantially Protestant, the United States saw major waves of Roman Catholic Irish and French Canadian immigration. Revival meetings spurred the growth of evangelical Methodists and Baptists. More radical groups such as the Shakers, Mormons, and Perfectionists emerged, each building its own churches.

In the early nineteenth century some Americans became caught up in the Greek War of Independence against the Turks. This contributed to a mania for classical culture, and Americans began to question why a liberated, democratic nation should follow the architectural precedents of England, the very country from which it had wrested its freedom. As a result, Americans began to build in the Greek Revival style and to worship in churches based on the temple-front motifs of classical architecture.

The temple front might be a full monumental portico in the Doric, Ionic, or Corinthian orders. It might

As the Romantic movement stirred a popular fascination for the Middle Ages, clergymen began to object to the use of "pagan" Greek Revival architecture for church design. The Gothic Revival style employed medieval church details to build contemporary churches. The Chapel at University of Virginia, Charlottesville, Virginia.

also be done on the cheap, with a shallow gable-front façade. Such churches were always painted plain white, in an attempt to imitate the look of bare classical stonework.

As in England, the nineteenth century and the Industrial Revolution saw a rise in the United States in romantic feelings for a medieval past. The Gothic Revival,

with its irregular, vertical, and romantic forms, was enthusiastically embraced by Episcopalian and Catholic parishes. Lesser revivals of the Romanesque and Renaissance styles also garnered favor. As in the original Gothic design, stone construction, flying buttresses, towers, and pointed arched windows are important design elements.

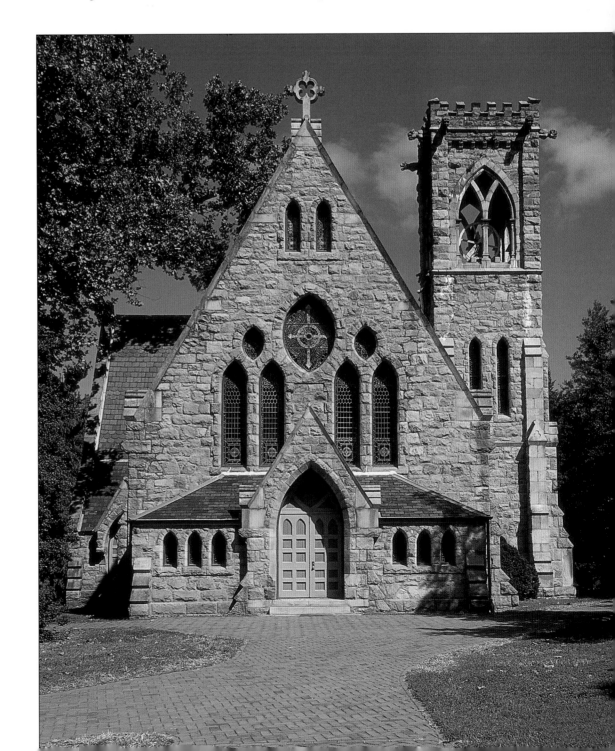

ABOVE: *Small communities often erect churches that reflect the concerns of their residents. Here, a statue of the Virgin Mary holding a fishing trawler tops a Catholic church in the fishing community of Gloucester, Massachusetts.* OPPOSITE: *Interior of a Catholic church with side aisles, wall dormers breaking the vaulted roof, and a domed apse at the chancel. Lille, Maine.*

While the aesthetic is handcrafted, such churches were (and are) often built of machined materials. These were largely the churches of the growing middle class in America.

In the decades following the American Civil War, in the late nineteenth century, clergymen witnessed the society around them in turmoil.

LEFT: *From antebellum times, churches were segregated in the rural South. Black Baptist churches furnished the nucleus for leadership from among their clergy and women's groups during the Civil Rights movement of the 1950s and 1960s. Interior, College Grove Baptist Church, LSU Rural Life Museum, Baton Rouge, Louisiana.* BELOW: *Exterior, College Grove Baptist Church, LSU Rural Life Museum, Baton Rouge, Louisiana.*

The fast growth of urban areas and the rise of industry, the flood of immigrants, the changing of rural traditions and domestic values, increasing confrontations between labor and business, scientific and technological development, and the general acceptance of Darwinism, threatened organized religion, as did the materialism of the Gilded Age. In urban areas, church buildings expanded to include lecture rooms and childcare facilities. Catholic congregations reacted to what they regarded as the evangelizing of their children in public schools by setting up parochial schools on a massive scale. It is also in this period that many Protestant communities saw Catholic churches built by immigrant congregations of laborers.

As in Europe, however, despite all these pressures toward fragmentation and erosion, on the whole rural congregations have retained considerable vigor in many parts of the country.

Today many churches and parishes are consolidated, and many old churches have become real estate offices, boutiques, and private residences. Yet the rapid development of rural land has also spurred an historic preservation movement that documents and protects thousands of churches.

Country Churches in Canada

The key to considering the rural churches of Canada, as with the nation itself, is diversity. Churches of every denomination represent the many peoples who have found a home in this country: the indigenous Indians, the French who came in the sixteenth century, the English who settled in the eighteenth, and Eastern European, Baltic, and Scandinavian immigrants of the nineteenth and twentieth centuries. English settlers and Ukrainian immigrants shared a common desire to bring something of the homes they had left behind to a new and unfamiliar place.

The French, who were the first Europeans to settle in the Canadian wilderness, included many Jesuit

Churches also lend themselves to individual whimsy, as in this tiny chapel straddling the United States–Canada border.

priests on missions to convert the Abanaki, Huron, and Iroquois. During the eighteenth century, Protestant English colonists launched their own missions to the Native Americans. Jesuits won over many Native peoples to Catholicism

Churches define a place, and then are defined by their place. A log construction Catholic church, decorated with Native American geometric designs, Wyoming.

by living among them, learning their languages, and adapting their religion to accommodate Native symbolism and culture, much as Christian evangelists had done in the conversion of Northern Europe one thousand years earlier.

In the armed conflicts with England that followed, known among the English as the French and Indian Wars, some Jesuit priests acted as military as well as spiritual leaders. While many Huguenots—French Protestants

who were a despised minority in France—settled in the Quebec region, New France was, like its mother country, strongly Catholic.

Following the end of the French and Indian Wars, the 1763 Treaty of Paris, the 1791 British Constitutional

Act, and the sale of the Louisiana Territory, Canada was split into two sections, with Upper Canada (mostly today's Ontario) English-speaking and Protestant, and Lower Canada (Quebec and the maritime provinces) French-speaking and Catholic. The Catholic religion was a powerful force for cultural identity among the French Canadians as they were subsequently stripped of economic and political power under British Crown rule.

Lower Canadian settlement patterns are based on the early seigniorial system of farm grants. Narrow strip fields extend inland from a river to a road. Small farm houses and outbuildings dot the roadside. A steepled church, often grandly rebuilt in the nineteenth century, dominates the flat farmland. It is not atypical for one such village church to be seen and heard from its neighboring village. The typical village church of the late eighteenth and early nineteenth centuries has an austere exterior and a highly decorated Baroque interior.

In Upper Canada, the spread of contemporary styles from England is evident in the many Gothic Revival–style churches employing

This Gothic Revival style church on Canada's Prince Edward Island would be at home in rural France. St. Mary's Church, Indian River.

ABOVE: *Sir Clifford Sifton, Canadian Minister of Interior, convinced many Eastern Europeans to migrate to Western Canada around the turn of the century. Ukrainian Catholic Church of the Virgin Mary, West Bend, Saskatchewan.* RIGHT *Ascension of Our Lord Russian Orthodox Church, Kodiak Island, Alaska.*

pinnacles, pointed arched windows, and buttresses. Such churches are often of the typical, wood-framed, symmetrical Anglo-American church forms: a gabled front nave with an attached tower projecting from the channel. But these essentially classical church forms are then decorated with the pinnacles, buttresses, pointed arch windows, and battlements that refer back to the Gothic churches of old Europe.

As the vast interior of Canada was opened up, many immigrants from north and east Europe resettled on the windswept prairies. The pattern of settlement was such that farmers built on their land and lived in isolation. A small church was the single social institution, and often the first wood-framed building erected in these communities. This wave of immigrants—Russians, Ukrainians, Poles, Hungarians,

Rumanians, and Germans—introduced new denominations, such as the Russian Orthodox and Ukrainian Catholic Churches, that changed the face of the prairie. The onion-domed, Byzantine-style church is as familiar a prairie architectural symbol as the railside grain elevator. Together these two buildings tell much about the nature of their communities.

An Easter procession outside the Ukrainian Catholic Church of the Virgin Mary, West Bend, Sasketchewan.

ABOVE: *Log churches were built across Canada, from Prince Edward Island to the Yukon Territory. Arcadian Pioneer Village, Mount Carmel, Prince Edward Island.*
LEFT: *This rough-board Gothic Revival Church has a domed apse with pointed arch windows, and a wood stove for heat. St. Savior's Anglican Church, Barkersville, British Columbia.* OPPOSITE PAGE: *Lovingly built upon the founding of a frontier community, churches were often abandoned when prospects waned or a gold rush beckoned. Relic church near Gimli, Manitoba.*

Chapter 6

Country Churches of Latin America

The Spanish Conquistadors who colonized South and Central America were exceptionally self-righteous about their holiness and the rightness of their mission, partly as a result of their long and recent struggle to expel the Moslem Moors from Spain and reestablish Christianity there. One Spanish soldier who served with Hernán Cortés in the conquest of Mexico wrote that he and his fellows had come "to serve God and His majesty, to give light to those who were in darkness, and to grow rich as all men desire to do."

Following Columbus' discovery of the Americas in 1492, Spanish adventurers arrived seeking gold, God, and glory. Taking over the Caribbean islands, they worked their way to the mainlands of Central America and South America. In 1519 five hundred Spanish soldiers led by Cortés attacked the Aztecs in their capital city of Tenochtitlán. In 1532 Francisco Pizarro invaded the land of the Incas in present-day Peru. In a shockingly brief span of time, two great native empires fell to the Spanish. Firearms, horses, steel blades, European diseases, and the Conquistadors' terrible sense of purpose, as well as civil war among the native peoples of both lands, aided this conquest.

The Conquistadors, Franciscans, and Dominicans who settled the far-flung Spanish empire in the New World brought with them the architecture of their native Spain and adapted it to the conditions they met in the Americas. The Spaniards' main preoccupation in Mexico and Latin America, as in the Spanish territories of North America, was to replace native temples with their own churches, often on the same site.

The monks and soldiers who settled Spain's far-flung empire in the New World brought with them the architecture of their homeland and adapted it to the conditions of the Americas. This brightly colored mission church is in El Triunfo, Baja California, Mexico.

The Spanish missionaries of the sixteenth and seventeenth centuries were successful in converting the Indians of the Americas by adopting Christianity to pre-Hispanic worship practices. The old gods were re-assigned saints' names, and festivals and ceremonies were worked into the liturgical calendar, often with

ABOVE: *Unlike sections of the North American frontier, churches were sited on the plazas and town centers of New Spain. The Church at El Fuerte, Sinaloa, Mexico, seen through the Plazuela Municipal.* LEFT: *A Baroque hall church with gabled belfry façade and elaborate entrance portico, in the town plaza at Copper Canyon. Chihuahua, Mexico.*

little modification. In saints' festivals, the Day of the Dead, Christmas, Easter, and the pre-Lenten Carnival are the remnants of pre-Hispanic fertility and other seasonal rites.

Colonists usually build in the style and manner of their mother country, and Spanish colonists were chiefly influenced by Gothic and Renaissance architecture. These two styles are sometimes worked together in sixteenth-century mission churches in Mexico. The Renaissance style in Mexico is called Plateresque, from the word *platero* for "silversmith," because it resembles the ornate inscribed decoration of silver work to be found on the front façades of churches in this style, accentuating the entrance portal. A round arched doorway flanked by columns or pilasters and rich stone carving are typical.

A soaring Gothic Revival cathedral with flat geometric applique decoration, including the Rose design in the second stage of the bell tower, and crocheted pinnacles crowning each buttress. Quetzaltenango, Guatemala.

ABOVE: *A unique marriage of masterful and intricate indigenous carving with the Baroque style decorates every inch of the surface of the façade of this seventeenth-century cathedral. Zacatecas, Mexico.*
RIGHT: *A baroque entrance portal with shallow, carved decoration and fluted pilasters marks the doorway of the Oratorio of San Felipe Neri, c. 1712. Town of San Miguel de Allende, Guanajuato, Mexico.*

decorated altar pieces are a common interior feature. In its wildest phase, Baroque style in Mexico developed into a form known as Churrigueresque, for a Spanish architect, Jose Benito de Churriguera. This style features even more elaborate surface decoration and the use of the estipite, a slender pilaster constructed with the wide part on top, creating an

Influences from Moorish Spain were also brought across the Atlantic and can be seen in the Muddejar style, which features highly carved wooden ceilings, as well as the use of exterior tiles. Baroque architecture, which came to the Spanish colonies in the seventeenth century, employs curving shapes and a greater use of color and ornamentation in general. Also, huge, highly

ABOVE: *In its most fanciful phase, the Baroque style developed into a form called Churrigueresque which featured greater elaboration of surface decoration and the estipite, a slender column with the narrower section at the base, for a topsy-turvy effect. Interior of San Antonio Church, Tiradentes, Brazil.* RIGHT: *Bell atop church of San Rafael, Town of San Miguel de Allende, Guanajuato, Mexico.*

"upside down" effect. Village churches at Tonantzintla and Acctepec, near Cholula in Puebla, Mexico, have rich, colorful interiors painted with flowers, birds, saints, and devils. This is an example of Indian artistic sensibility applied to Christian themes.

A hallmark of Mexican mission architecture, very rare outside of Mexico, is the *capilla abierta,* or "open chapel." Missions were typically fortified, and featured a church, cloister, and outbuildings arranged in a hollow square or rectangle, with the buildings forming some of the exterior walls. The churchyard had a capilla abierta where mass could be offered to large groups of Indians while the church was being constructed. This may also be an attempt on the part of monks to imitate the pre-Christian outdoor ceremonies with which the native peoples were familiar.

An important aspect of the Baroque style was its use of theatrical setting and illusion to create an emotional connection between viewer and view. Use of lighting and surrounds of carved putae and foliage that overlap the main scene were typical, as in this interior detail from San Antonio Church. Tiradentes, Brazil.

ABOVE: *The Missionaries were successful in converting the Indians of the Americas by adapting pre-Hispanic worship practices. Old gods were assigned saints' names, and festivals and ceremonies were worked into the liturgical calendar. This seventeenth-century Copper Canyon mission church has an added bell tower. Chihuahua, Mexico.* RIGHT: *Seventeenth-century mission church at Creel Cusarare, Chihuahua, Mexico.*

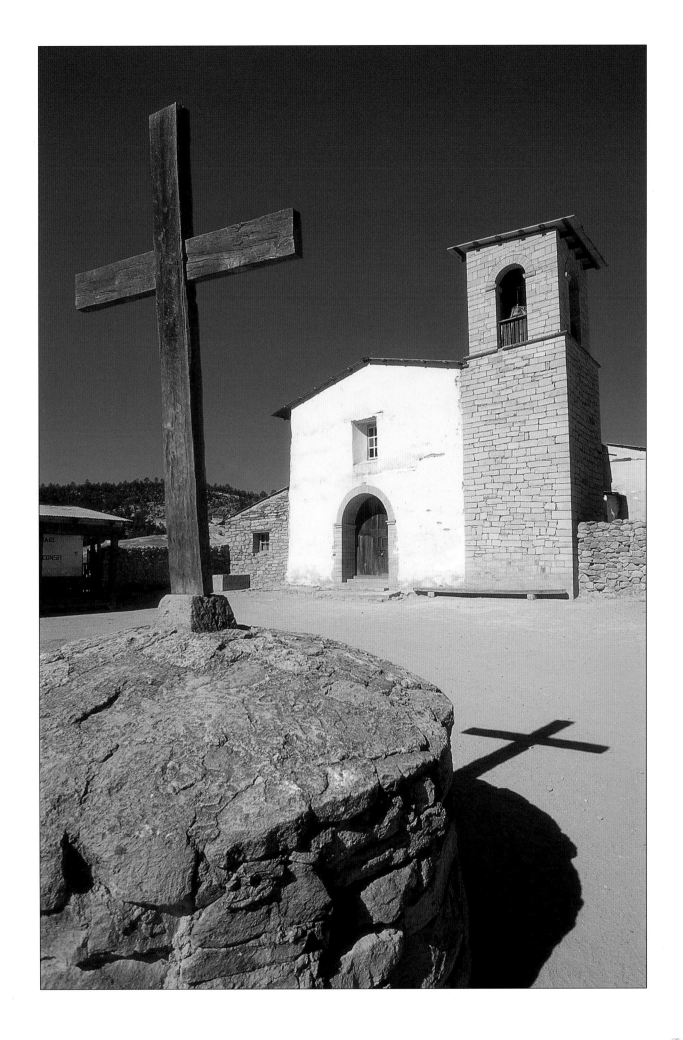

ABOVE: *The carved altar screen at the Sanctuario de Nuestra Señora de Esquipulas. Built in 1816, the Sanctuario is a pilgrimage shrine where thousands come each year to seek divine intercession and healing. Chimayo, New Mexico.* OPPOSITE TOP: *A striking feature of this mission is the long, high nave with ceiling carried on exposed beams, and side wall and window borders embellished with bold geometric motifs by native artists. Creel Cusarare, Mexico.* OPPOSITE BOTTOM: *Requests for divine intervention at Cata Church, Guanajuato, Mexico.*

In 1767 the Jesuit order was blamed for a general economic decline, and was expelled from Latin America. During the Wars of Independence that followed Napoleon's conquest of Spain and Portugal in 1807–1808, the Church sided with the land-owning aristocracy. Between 1818 and 1825, Simón Bolívar and his supporters liberated northern and western South America. In this period, every territory in South and Central America except Cuba and Puerto Rico won their independence.

Although the official Church hierarchy tended to side with the aristocracy during this time of upheaval, on a local level numerous parish priests sided with their parishioners. Father Miguel Hidalgo led the Mexican people in the first War of Independence in 1810 under a banner of the Virgin of Guadeloupe. When he was executed, another parish priest, Father Jose Maria Morelos, took over the group's leadership.

South of Mexico, in rural Central and South America, churches today are very plain inside and out, though the altar piece may be ornate, decorated with beautiful vernacular interpretations of the Crucifixion or a patron saint's life. In Mexico and in the highlands of Guatemala,

ABOVE: *Baroque Church of Chamula, seen across its plaza at Chiapas, Mexico.* RIGHT: *El Calvario Church, City of Cobain, Guatemala.*

Bolivia, and Peru, country parishes cover wide areas. One striking example is the village of Tzicatlan, which has a small church consisting of a single room, though its entrance is flanked by two simple bell towers. This church's parish contains thirty-five villages, linked only by rough jeep tracks and mule paths. The parish priest covers the 900 square miles (1440km) of his isolated community by mule, carrying simple medicines in his saddlebag because there are no doctors.

As in so many others around the world, in the poor rural villages of South America and Central America, the church ceremonies— baptism, first communion, confirmation, marriage, and last rites—are still the significant rites of passage in the journey through life. Today, the church remains the unifying force that it was when Latin America was part of the Spanish empire.

Typical rural church design, central nave with flanking bell towers displays the scale of human endeavor measured against the surrounding landscape. Jujuy Province, Argentina.

OPPOSITE: *In recent decades the evangelical Protestant faiths have made inroads into the traditionally Catholic populations of Central and South America. First Church, San Pedro La Laguna, Guatemala.*
ABOVE: *This diminutive chapel, built relatively recently along a lonely stretch of highway on the Baja peninsula, remains true to traditional form. Guerro Negro, Baja California, Mexico.*

Bibliography

Ahlstrom, Sydney E. *A Religious History of the American People.* New Haven: Yale University Press, 1972.

Banner, Robert. *Gothic Architecture.* New York: George Braziller, 1967.

Chadwick, Owen. *A History of Christianity.* New York: St. Martin's Press, 1995.

Jordon, R. Furneaux. *A Concise History of Western Architecture.* N.p.: England: Harcourt, Brace & World, Inc., 1969.

Kubach, Hans Erich. *Romanesque Architecture.* New York: Harry N. Abrams, Inc., 1975.

Saalman, Howard. *Medieval Architecture: European Architecture 600–1200.* New York: George Braziller, 1967.

Sitwell, Sacheverell. *Monks, Nuns and Monasteries.* New York: Holt, Rinehart & Winston, 1965.

Various. *Encyclopedia of World Art.* London: McGraw-Hill Book Co., 1968.

Index

Photography Credits

©John Elk III: pp. 17 bottom, 29, 53, 62, 94 both, 100 top, 104 both, 105, 110, 111, 113 top, 114 top, 116

FPG International: ©Josef Beck: p. 22; ©Haroldo Castro: p. 35; ©Walter Choroszewski: p. 1; ©Robert Cundy: p. 38; ©Dick Dietrich: p. 88 top; ©Jeri Gleiter: p. 100 bottom; ©Farrell Grehan: p. 66; ©Peter Gridley: p. 91; ©Michael Hart: p. 24 left; ©Lee Kuhn: pp. 5, 80, 112; ©Bill Losh: p. 83; ©Mike Malyszko: p. 21 left; ©Guy Marche: p. 14; ©Jonathan Meyers: pp. 81, 82 right; ©David Noble: p. 96; ©Fergus O'Brien: p. 34; ©H.G. Ross: p. 12; ©Ulf Sjostedt: p. 65; ©Ron Thomas: p. 28; ©August Upitis: p. 84; ©Karl & Jill Wallin: p. 36; ©Toyohiro Yamada: p. 85; ©A. Zalon: pp. 56–57

©Robert Fried: pp. 10, 11, 20, 21 right, 27, 54, 58, 72 both, 107, 108 bottom, 114 bottom

©The Irish Picture Library: p. 44

Leo de Wys, Inc.: ©Fridmar Damm: p. 67; ©Jon Hicks: p. 13; ©Don Pitcher: p. 98 right; ©Jose Fusta Raga: pp. 50–51; ©Steve Vidler: p. 55; ©Vladpans: p. 82 left

©Ken Murphy: p. 2

©Richard T. Nowitz Photography: pp. 46–47 both, 49, 59, 64

©Photri: pp. 26, 70, 73, 76, 77, 97

©Kay Shaw: pp. 37, 41, 43, 45

©Brian Vanden Brink: pp. 86, 87, 88 bottom, 90, 93

Woodfin Camp & Associates: ©Nubar Alexanian: p. 92; ©Craig Aurness: p. 89; ©Bernard Boutrit: pp. 15, 17 top, 24 right–25, 108 top, 109; ©Geoffrey Clifford: pp. 68, 115; ©Eastcott/Momatiuk: pp. 74, 98 left, 99, 101; ©F. Fournier: p. 16; ©Robert Frerck: pp. 52, 102-103, 113 bottom, 117; ©Anthony Howarth: pp. 33, 42; ©Catherine Karnow: pp. 60; ©Paula Lerner: pp. 6–7, 78–79; ©Chuck O'Rear: p. 71; ©A. Ramey: p. 3; ©Michael Sheil: endpapers, pp. 30–31; ©Mireille Vautier: p. 106; ©Adam Woolfitt: pp. 8–9, 18, 19, 23, 32, 39, 63, 75; ©Mike Yamashita: pp. 61, 95